Estimating Recreational Benefits of the Dhaka Zoo: An Individual Travel Cost Approach

Md. Mahmudul Hasan Chowdhury [1,*],
Dr. Syed Naimul Wadood [2]

ABSTRACT

This study estimates recreational benefits of the Dhaka Zoo by Individual Travel Cost Method (ITCM). The study estimates the benefits of operating the Zoo along with revealed visitors' willingness to pay to visit and enjoy the Zoo. The total annual consumer surplus from recreation of the Dhaka Zoo is estimated at approximately BDT 856.4 million (US$ 10.98 million). Study has found that Various factors influence the value visitors obtained from the Zoo; these include travel cost, household income and the environmental quality of the Dhaka Zoo. Improvements in the overall quality of the Zoo is likely to increase recreational benefits of the visitors and also visitation rates. The study recommends that current Dhaka Zoo entrance fee of BDT 20 per person could be adjusted every year. This would generate enough revenue to cover the operating and maintenance expenses of the Zoo.

Key words: Zoological Garden, Dhaka Zoo, Natural Resources, Non- Market Valuation, Recreational Benefits, Travel Cost, Individual Travel Cost Method,Consumer Surplus, Public Policy

[1] *Researcher, Master of Economics in Environmental Economics, Dhaka School of Economics, University of Dhaka.*
* *Corresponding Author: E-mail: imlewu@gmail.com*
[2] *Associate Professor, Departments of Economics, University of Dhaka.*

ACKNOWLEDGEMENT

We appreciate useful advice and support from all the faculty members of Dhaka School of Economics, with special mention for Dr. A K M Nazrul Islam, Associate Professor and Coordinator of Environmental Economics Program and Dr. Qazi Kholiquzzman Ahmad, Director of Dhaka School of Economics. Cooperation from the Dhaka Zoo authorities is also acknowledged.

Background

Established in 1974, main objectives of the Dhaka Zoological Garden (Dhaka Zoo) at Mirpur are wildlife conservation through collection and breeding of rare and endangered species of wild animals, research, education and recreation. It is also involved in conservation of wild animals and promotion of public awareness about these species. The zoo has a captive breeding program and has successfully bred the lion, the Royal Bengal Tiger, primates, deer leopard and many birds. About 3.9 million visitors visit Dhaka Zoo every year (Ref. zoo sources). It is a hub for healthy recreation of peoples of all ages. Peaceful environment of the zoo attracts people to get relief from the hustle and bustle of urban life. This is the only zoological garden in the city, therefore does not face any competition within this type of recreational location category.

It is the (publicly administered) national zoo under the Ministry of Fisheries and Livestock. Area of this zoo is approx. 75 hectares. It has two lakes of about 13 hectares which receive thousands of migratory birds every year in the winter season (see Annex). The total number of flora and fauna in the zoo is found to be approx. 2,150 of 191 species. In this research we aim to measure economic valuation of recreational benefits of this zoo, and additionally we would provide valuable information regarding the current condition of Dhaka Zoo and address the plausible role of goverment to improve various tourist services by creating improved and sustainable management practices.

The organization of the paper is as follows. While *Section 1* discusses the background, *Section 2* outlines the objectives of the study, and *Section 3* is an overview of the literature. *Section 4* discusses study methodology whereas *Section 5* discusses data. *Section 6* introduces survey findings and *Section 7* presents estimation results and follow-up calculations. *Section 8* concludes with policy recommendations.

1. Objectives of the Study

The main objective of the study was to measure the recreational value of the Dhaka Zoological Garden. The study aimed at finding out effective policy for development and better management, this broad objective segmented into some specific objectives as follows:

1) Whether there exists usual functional relationship between travel cost and zoo visitation rate;

2) To determine the factors that affect visitors' Willingness- to- Pay (WTP) for recreational services of the zoo;

3) To estimate the Consumer Surplus and the Recreational Value (Benefits) of the zoo;

4) Use these values to establish effective guideline and efficient policy option for the Dhaka Zoo.

3. Overview of the Literature

The common approaches used in the studies on valuing ecotourism and recreational sites are Travel Cost Method (TCM) and the Contingent Valuation Method (CVM). Whereas the CVM is a non-market based method, the TCM is a revealed preference approach for economic valuation of recreational sites. The Travel Cost Method (TCM) proposed by Hotelling (1947) is one of the oldest methods in the environmental resource valuation literature. It is a method based on observed behavior reflecting utility maximization subject to constraint(s) (Freeman, 1993). TCM estimates the consumer surplus (Marshallian), which approximates and is bounded by the compensating variation (CV) and the equivalent variation (EV) welfare measures (Brander *et al.,* 2006). According to TCM, if a consumer visits a recreational site, the benefits he receives should be more than or equal to the cost incurred although he does not pay a market-determined price. As such, this method uses the *travel cost* as a proxy for the price of recreation. Since the travel cost varies with distance from the recreational site, it is possible to derive a *"demand curve"* from the varying cost information. Based on this demand curve, it is possible to estimate the consumer surplus as a measure of welfare (Gunatilake, 2003). To note that perceived costs as reported by recreation site users are often considered as travel cost (Rolfe and Prabha, 2007).

TCM has two basic variants depending on the definition of the dependent variable: *Individual Travel Cost Method (ITCM)* which is appropriate for sites with high individual visitation rates and the *Zonal Travel Cost Method (ZTCM)* which is applicable for sites with very low individual visitation patterns (Rolfe and Prabha, 2007). Shammin (1999) used Zonal Travel Cost Method (ZTCM) to determine the willingness to pay (WTP) for Dhaka Zoo where the cost of visiting substitute sites were also taken into account. This study found yearly willingness to pay by consumers for the zoo to be around BDT 1,288 million. Nam and Son (2001) applied Individual Travel Cost Method (ITCM) to consider the number of visits of every single visitors. In this study the dependent variable was the quantity demanded, which was modeled as a function of the visitor's travel cost to the site and also some other economic and qualitative indicators. The suitable functional form for the *trip generating function* (TGF) is found to be varying across studies. Thusitha and Manoj (2010) discusses of Diyawanna Oya wetlands in the greater Colombo area which is of growing importance as a tourism site, and finds that this wetlands can generate an annual consumer surplus of

LKR 3,890 million or (USD 35 million) to people who use the area as a recreation site. Shinwary, Rahman and Uddin (2009) finds out which factors working as motives for visiting the Dhaka Zoo. They mentioned that zoos represented an opportunity for family-based trips in Dhaka city. Malakar, Khan and Chakraborty (2010) also attempt to identify and analyze the factors and causes that motivate visitors for visiting Dhaka Zoo. The study shows that toilet facilities, cleanness and facility of car parking are the most important factors for visiting Dhaka Zoo.

We note that ITCM has some advantages over ZTCM since it takes into account the inherent variation in the data compared to the aggregation and can be estimated using a smaller number of observations. Furthermore, ITCM is more flexible and can be applied to a wide range of sites (Khan, 2004) while eliciting rich information on visitors' characteristics, preferences and behavior. (Bowker and Leeworthy,1998) argue that researchers prefer ITCM over ZTCM for reasons such as statistical competence, theoretical consistency in modeling of individual behavior, the ability to avoid arbitrary zone definitions. However, the application of the suitable TCM depends on the identification of the dependent variable. Therefore, some studies use both methods (Rolfe and Prabha (2007); Nam *et al.*, (2005)). Scholars have extensively used TCM in natural resources related recreation research in order to value site access as well as changes in site quality in developed countries (Grigalunas *et al.*,

2004; Kealy *et al.*, 1986; Poor and Smith (2004)) whereas only a handful of valuation studies have used this method in developing countries, particularly in South Asia. While Gunatilake and Vieth (1998) applied ZTCM to estimate the recreational value of the Pinnawela Elephant Orphanage of Sri Lanka, Khan (2004) used ITCM to estimate the recreational benefits from the Margalla Hills National Park in Northern Pakistan where he estimated a hypothetical demand curve to assess the change in visitors' perceptions of improvements in the quality of amenities in the park.

.

4. Methodology

This study had employed ITCM to assess the benefits associated with recreation in the Dhaka Zoological garden .The ITCM is basically an extension of conventional household production function (HPF) models that treat the household as maximizing utility based on consumption and production decisions. The ITCM enables an assessment of individual preferences for the consumption of non-marketed goods. The principle technique of ITCM is to estimate a 'trip generating function' where the visitation rate depends on the cost of travel to the study site, travel costs to close substitute sites, and other socioeconomic and demographic characteristics of the visitors (Willis and Garrod , 1999).

Since the Dhaka Zoo is an urban zoo that is located close to the smaller cities around Dhaka (i.g., Saver, Gazipur and Tongi) a majority of visitors are from nearby areas. The ITCM has a distinct advantage over the ZTCM in that it also takes into account the inherent variation in the data, rather than relying on zonal aggregate data. For an accurate travel perspective, the ITCM has the advantage as its trip generating function can be estimated using a smaller number of observations than is the case with the ZTCM (Willis and Garrod, 1999).

5. Data

The study required primary data and it was collected by conducting a structured questionnaire survey of face-to-face interviews. Some other form of information, such as official documents and other related literature regarding the Dhaka Zoo, was collected from the Information and Curator Office of the Zoo, Bangladesh Bureau of Statistics (BBS), Ministry of Fisheries and Livestock.

5.1 Sample Size and Sampling

The ITCM requires information about the visitors to a recreational site (Frank A.Ward and Beal, 2000). This information collected by conducting an on-site survey of visitors to the Dhaka Zoo. We use systematic sampling. Average number of visitors in Dhaka Zoo (per day) approximate 11,000. We took 10 interviews each day of the earliest visitors, randomly selecting one person from the earliest 5, then continuing with a 4 person gap in-between (such as 3rd, 8th and 13th, etc.). We assumed marginal error to be at 5%, level of confidence 95%, and response distribution 85% (which was determined from pilot survey of on 20 visitors). Dhaka Zoo statistics provide yearly visitation rate in Dhaka Zoo approximately **3,443,000** by deducting 52 administrative holidays of Zoo. We used the formula below for sample size determination. The sample size n and margin of error E are given by:

$$X = Z(c/100)^2 \; r \; (100\text{-}r), \quad n = N \, x / \, ((N\text{-}1) \, E^2 + x), \quad E = Sqrt \; [(N-n) \, x/_n \, (N\text{-}1)]$$

Where N is the population size, r is the fraction of responses those are interested in, and $Z(c/100)$ is the critical value for the confidence level c. We get minimum recommended sample size 196, rounded to 200 visitors. Survey was conducted both weekdays and weekends. The survey was conducted in July and August of year 2013.

5.2 Study Design

We use linear regression model, since this is a standard practice to report OLS regression as a starting point. We applied censored regression model, cause in our study we set a criteria at least one visit in Zoo last 12 months period. We applied Tobit regression model (left censored). We noted and reported the marginal effects of the Tobit model result. The marginal effects show how the probabilities of the outcome change with respect to changes in regressors. The responses to the structured questions were analyzed with the help of statistical software STATA V. 12 and SPSS.

5.3 Theoretical Framework

In order to model the travel cost function, we follow Freeman (1993) and assume that the individual's utility depends on the total time spent at the site (the Dhaka Zoological garden, in this instance), the environmental quality of the Zoo, and the quantity of the numeraire. With the duration of the visit fixed for simplicity, the time on site can be represented by the number of visits. The individual solves the following utility maximizing problem:

Max: U (X, r, q) . . . .
(1)

Subject to the twin constraints of monetary and time budgets:

$M + P_w . t_w = X + c.r$ . . . .
(2)

$$t^* = t_w + (t_1 + t_2)r \quad \dots\dots\dots\dots\dots\dots\dots\dots\dots\dots\dots\dots\dots \quad (3)$$

Where X = the quantity of numeraire whose price is one,

r = number of visits to the Dhaka Zoological garden,

q = environmental quality at the site,

M = exogenous income,

P_w = wage rate,

c = monetary cost of a trip,

t^* = total discretionary time,

t_w = hours worked,

t_1 = round-trip travel time, and

t_2 = time spent on site.

It is assumed that r and q are (weak) complements in the utility function, implying that the number of visits will be an increasing function of the site's environmental quality. The time constraint reflects the fact that both travel to the site and time spent on the site take time away from other activities. Thus there is an opportunity cost to the time spent in the recreation activity. We also assume that the individual is free to choose the amount of time spent at work and that work does not convey utility (or disutility) directly. Thus the opportunity cost of time is the wage rate. Finally, we also assume that the monetary cost of a trip to the site has two components: the entry fee f, which could be zero, and the monetary cost of travel. This cost of travel is $P_d \cdot d$, where P_d is the per-kilometer cost of travel and d is the distance to the site and return from it.

Substituting equation (3) into (2) yields:

$$M + P_{w} \cdot t^* = X + P_{r} \cdot r \ldots \ldots \ldots \ldots \ldots \ldots \ldots \ldots \ldots \ldots$$

(4)

Where P_r is the full price of a visit, which is the sum of entry fee (f, which could be zero), P_d is the per (km) cost of travel and d is the distance in km as shown in equation….. (5).

$$P_r = c + P_w (t_1 + t_2) = f + P_d \cdot d + P_w (t_1 + t_2) \ldots \ldots \ldots \ldots \ldots$$

(5)

As equation (5) makes clear, the full price of a visit consists of four components: the entry fee, the monetary cost of travel to the site, the time cost of travel to the site, and the cost of time spent at the site. On the assumption that individuals are free to choose the number of hours worked at a given wage rate, the two time costs are valued at the wage rate.

Maximizing equation (1) subject to the constraint of equation (4) will yield the individual's demand functions for visits:

$$r = r (P_r, M, q) \ldots \ldots \ldots \ldots \ldots \ldots \ldots \ldots \ldots \ldots \ldots$$

(6)

The data on rates of visitation, travel costs, and variation in entry fees (if any) can be used to estimate the coefficient on P_r in a travel cost-visitation function. Because of the linearity of equation (5), the coefficient on P_r can be used to derive the individual's demand for visits to a site as a function of the entry fee.

Monetary cost of a trip to a site has two types of costs i.e.

$C = f + P_d \cdot d$ Where, f = Entry fee (can be even 0)

P_d = Per Km Travel Cost

d = distance (round trip distance)

Using the Lagrangian multiplier, we can get an equation which can be used for further algebraic manipulation,

$L = U(X, r, q) + \pi [(M + P_w \cdot t^*) - \{X + r (f + P_d \cdot d + P_w \cdot (t_1 + t_2))\}]$

Using partial derivatives, we can generate three equations as below:

$U_x (X, r, q) = \pi$

$U_r (X, r, q) = \pi (f + P_d \cdot d + P_w \cdot (t_1 + t_2))$ and

$M + P_w \cdot t^* = X + r [f + P_d \cdot d + P_w \cdot (t_1 + t_2)]$

After further algebraic calculations we get the following equation:

$r = r (P_r, M, q)$,   where 'r' is the number of visits

$P_r = f + P_d \cdot d + P_w \cdot (t_1 + t_2)$

Here, $r = r (Pr, M, q)$ represents the demand function 'r' i.e. the number of visits to the site. Economic valuation of a recreation site requires the estimation of the demand for recreation.

Once we get the demand equation we can easily calculate the *Consumer Surplus (CS)* using integral calculus:

$CS = \int^{r*} r (P_r, M, q) \, d_r - P_r^* \, r$

3.2.1 Trip Generating Function (TGF)

As suggested by Garrod and Willis (1999), Trip Generating Function is used to generate a regression model for estimation. The trip generating function for the present study is set as:

$$V_{ij} = f(TC_{ij}, Q_i, S_i, Y_i)$$

In our model, the number of trips per year made to Dhaka Zoo by each individual is represent by *r*. various independent variables are used to explain variation in the dependent variable *beta* .Both economic theory and the considerable experience of recreation managers have shown that demographic and other independent variables influence recreation visitation to one side with demographic variables, are the most important variables including travel cost, travel time, site quality and congestion.

5.4 Econometric Model

Economic theory does not suggest any particular functional form for Travel Cost Methods. But most common practice is to statistically test various functional forms such as:

1) **Linear** $r = \alpha + \beta P$
2) **Log linear** $\log r = \alpha + \beta P$
3) **Double-log** $\log r = \alpha + \log \beta P$
4) **Negative exponential** $r = \alpha + \log \beta P$

The estimated consumer surplus for an individual making revisits to the site in case of a linear form is given by $CS = -1/\beta_1$
* Where, CS= Average Consumer Surplus from a visit to site 'j' for individual 'i': β_1= Co-efficient of TC_{ij}

The linear functional form implies finite visits at zero cost and has a critical cost above which the model predicts negative visits (Garrods and Willis, 1999). The consumer surplus in case of the log-linear functional form is given by CS= **-1/ β_1.** It implies a finite number of visits at a zero cost and never predicts negative visits, even at a very high cost (Garrod and Willis, 1999). We used linear functional form for our study.

The econometric specification used in this study depicts the number of visits to Dhaka Zoological garden as a function of factors such as the travel cost, time spent in traveling, income, education, age, sex, family size, site quality, employment status, etc. Thus, the model is defined as follows:

r_i *= β_0 + β_1 travel cost + β_2 household income + β_3 age of Visitor + β_4 visitor's highest level of education + $\beta_5$household size+ $\beta_6 D_1$(dummy)gender*

+ $\beta_7 D_2$(dummy)Zoo environmental quality+$\beta_8 D_3$(dummy)Govser +$\beta_9 D_4$(dummy)Selfemp_busi +$\beta_{10} D_5$(dummy)Pvt_serv +e_i

-- where **r_i**, the dependent variable, stands for the number of visits by the ith individual to the Dhaka Zoo in the last 12 months time period, travel cost means round trip total cost from an individual's residence to and from the site and includes the opportunity cost of travel time and stay at Zoo.

6. Discussions of the Survey Findings

Findings from the survey are discussed with the help of tables, charts, diagrams and figures. Data analysis begins with calculation of descriptive statistics of the variables. These statistics summarize various aspects about the data, giving details about the sample and also try to provide information about the population (visitors) from which the sample was drawn.

Table 1 Descriptive Statistics

Variables	Mean	Minimum	Maximum
Round trip cost of visitors to Dhaka Zoo (in BDT)	47	21.5	640
Distance (Km)	17.5	1	400
Number of trips to Dhaka Zoo during the last 12 months (including this one)	3	1	7
Age (Years) of respondent	23.52	16	40
Visitors spend on their trip (food) (in BDT)	100	10	480
Visitors spend on their trip (soft drinks) (in BDT)	80	48	300
Monthly salary of respondent visitors (in BDT)	20,308	2000	2,00,000
Household Size	4.78	1	12

N=200

The Table 1 provides a summary of the descriptive statistics of recreational behavior, the demographic characteristics, and travel cost information of the sample of visitors to the Dhaka Zoo. On average, from the respondent's visitors we had found average visits to Dhaka Zoo was 3 times a year, whereas we found maximum visit 7 times and minimum 1 time in last one year.

Table 2 Descriptive Characteristics of Sample Respondents (Dichotomous)

Variables	Percent	
Gender	76.50 (Male)	23.50 (Female)
Marital Status	21.50 (Single)	78.50 (Married)
If there were no other sources of funding available would you be willing to pay higher entry fee?	51.50 (Yes)	48.50 (No)
What is your perception about environmental quality of the Zoo?	45.50 Good)	54.50 (Bad)
N=200		

The Table 2 above exhibits that, in the sample we have found 76.5 percent were male and 23.5 percent were female. Between those nearly 79 percent found single and 21 percent found married. We tried to know about visitors' perception about environmental quality where nearly 55 respondents said environmental quality of zoo was "bad" and only 45 percent responded that it was "good". We tried to know about their opinions for financing the Dhaka Zoo improvement, where the question was- "if there were no other source of funding available would you be willing to pay higher entry fee?" Opinions were divided as 52 per cent responded "yes" whereas 48 per cent said "no".

Table 3 Frequency Distribution of Household Monthly Income

Income Groups (BDT/Month)	No. of Households	Percent
Upto 5,000	1	0.50
5,000 to 10,000	8	4.00
10,000 to 20,000	21	10.50
20,000 to 30,000	80	40.00
30,000 to 50,000	69	34.50
50,000 to 1,00,000	17	8.50
More than Tk. 1,00,000	4	2.00
Total	**200**	**100**

The Table 3 above exhibits that around 75 per cent of the respondents belonged to families whose monthly income was in between BDT 20,000 to 50,000, with small tails on both sides of the distribution.

Table 4 Respondents' Mode of Transport (Percentage)

Mode of Transport-Arrival	Percent	Mode of Transport-Return	Percent
Train	0.50	Train	0.50
Bus	33	Bus	33
Private Vehicle	1.50	Private Vehicle	1.50
Rickshaw	50.50	Rickshaw	51.50
Combination	14.50	Combination	13.00
Total	**100**	**Total**	**100**

Table 4 above shows that we found about 50 per cent of the respondents' mode of transport was rickshaw, 33 per cent of the respondents' travel by bus and close to 14 per cent respondents used some combination as modes of transport.

Table 5 Respondents' Level of Education

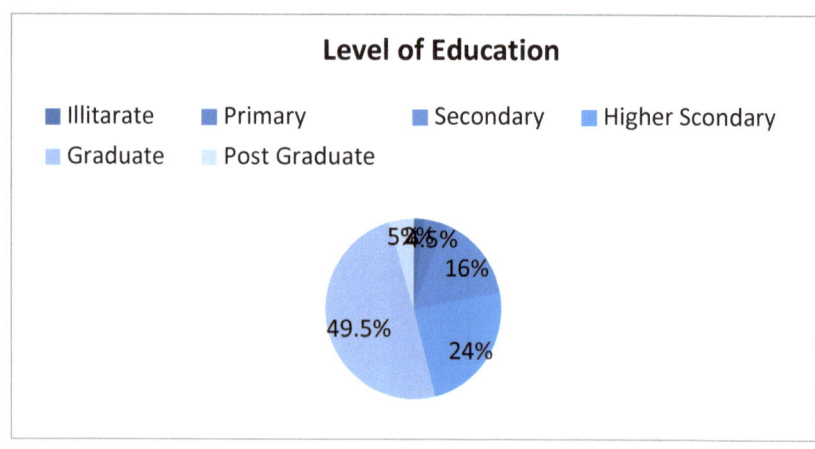

Table 5 exhibits that only 2 per cent respondents were illiterate whereas close up to 50 per cent were graduates.

Table 6 Classification of the Sample Respondents by Occupation

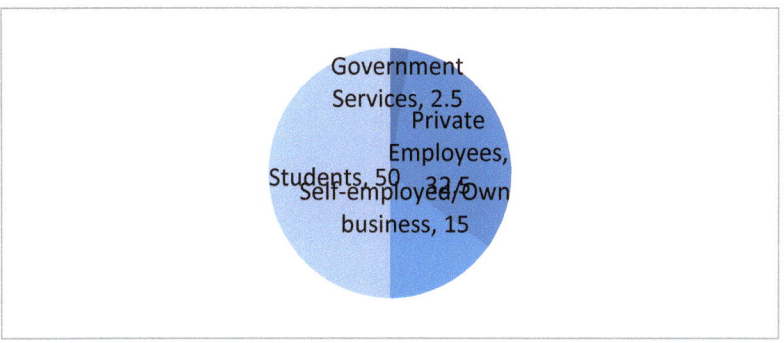

Table 6 exhibits that 50 per cent respondents were students, nearly 33 per cent were private employees, 15 per cent were self-employed/own business categories.

7. Empirical Results

Table 7 below reports the results of the travel cost regression models from the linear regression specification (the dependent variable is last 12 months' visitation rate (including this one)).

Table 7 Estimated Results of Linear Regression

Independent Variables	Estimated Coefficients	t	P>|t|
Travel Cost	-.0035759***	-3.46	0.001
Age	-.0789237**	-3.02	0.003
Monthly Income of Household (MHI)	.2568437***	2.81	0.006
Household Size (HHS)	.0001476	0.00	0.998
Level of Education	.0047646	0.20	0.844
Gender (1 for Male, 0 for Female)	.068669	0.30	0.767
Environmental Quality (1 for Good, Others 0)	.3818645**	1.96	0.042
Govser (1 for Govser, Others 0)	-.1430433	-0.34	0.733
Selfemp_busi (1 for Selfemp_busi, Others 0)	.1445064	0.45	0.655
Pvt_serv (1 for Pvt_serv ,Others 0)	.1723749	0.82	0.412
Constant	3.441933	4.21	0.000

$F(10, 189) = 5.38$
$Prob > F = 0.0000$
R-squared = 0.1756
N= 200

Notes: ***$P<0.01$, **$P<0.05$, *$P<0.1$
Robust coefficicent estimates due to heteroscedasticity problem

For every unit increase in Travel Cost we expect (-.0035759) point decrease in visitation rate, controlling for all other variables, and this is statistically negatively significant at 1% level. Age of the respondent, monthly household income and environmental quality of the zoo are found to be statistically significant and with expected signs.

People of younger age pay more frequent visits to Dhaka Zoo, respondents are expected to visit more of their monthly household income are higher, and respondents are to make more frequent visits to the zoo if they find the environmental quality to be good.

We used *Censored Regression Model*, which commonly arise in econometrics in cases where the variable of interest is only observable under certain conditions. In this study we set a criteria at least 1 visit to to last 12 months periods. As we know model commonly used to deal with censored data is the Tobit model. To note that we used left-censored Tobit regression model here (since one is the minimum that (including this visit)) that is reported.

Table 8 Marginal Effects of the Explanatory Variables

Independent Variables	dy/dx	z	P>|z|
Travel Cost	-.0201626**	-2.85	0.004
Age	-.1155451***	-3.42	0.001
Monthly Income of household (MHI)	.3544174**	3.16	0.002
Household Size (HHS)	-.0017929	-0.02	0.981
Level of Education	.0083618	0.30	0.764
Gender(1 for Male ,0 for Female)	.0348301	0.14	0.888
Environmental Quality (1 for Good, Others 0)	.3926534**	1.82	0.049
Govser (1 for Govser, Others 0)	-.0802718	-0.14	0.891
Selfemp_busi (1 for Selfemp_busi, Others 0)	.3385507	0.92	0.356

Pvt_serv (1 for Pvt_serv, Others 0)	.3507818	1.49	0.136

Note: dy/dx for factor levels is the discrete change from the base level.
***P<0.01; **P<0.05, *P<0.10

Marginal effect on the latent variable

The marginal coefficients in Table 8 show that keeping the influences of other factors constant at their mean value, a one per cent increase in independent variable has a statistically significant change in dependent variable.The estimated coefficient TC (Travel Cost) is found statistically significant at 5% level. For every unit increase in TC we expect that the probability of 2 per cent decrease in zoo visitation rates.

Cost-benefit (Social) analysis of Dhaka Zoo

Total number of visitors in Dhaka Zoo (per year) is 3,443,000 approx[1]. Where average number of visitors in Dhaka Zoo (per day) 11,000 approximate[1]. Zoo ticket price was BDT 20 in year 2013, According to this yearly revenue generate from gate tickets was $(3,443,000 \times 20) = 68,860,000$ or BDT 68.86 Million***. Average *Consumers Surplus* based on this study is $CS = \dfrac{-1}{-.0035759} = 279.64$*

Total Consumers Surplus based on this study is

962,800,520 approx[2].Net Consumers Surplus is (9,62,800,520 - 68,860,000) = 8, 93,940,520 or (893.94052 Million) .Net Social Surplus is 893.94052 Million (Social Benefit) - 37.5 million ** (Social Cost) = 856.44052 million.

---

* According to suggested formula by Garrod & Willis (1999) Consumers Surplus CS= -1/ β_1 * Where, CS= Average Consumer Surplus from a visit to site 'j' by individual 'i β_1= Co-efficient of TC ij (See Table 8)

** The yearly budget of Dhaka Zoo is Tk 37.5 million, out of which BDT 25 million is spent on feeding the animals (2012).

*** Yearly revenue generate from gate tickets.

[1] Every Sunday Dhaka Zoo remain closed if not festival day i.e. (Eid, Puja/Victory day, etc) so we calculate (11,000×313) by deducting 52 holidays of Zoo (source: Dhaka Zoo curator office statistics).

[2] TCS= CS x Total Number of Visitors to Dhaka Zoo in Last One Year.

Willingness-to-pay

In this study we used open bid system to determine willingness to pay for Zoo visit among visitors.

Table 9 Correlations among Household Monthly Income and Willingness to Pay Bidding

	Household Monthly Income	WTP-30	WTP-40	WTP-50	WTP-60	More than WTP-60
Household Monthly Income	1.0000					
WTP-30	-0.1131	1.0000				
WTP-40	-0.1842	0.5620	1.0000			
WTP-50	-0.1791	0.3866	0.6879	1.0000		
WTP-60	-0.0823	0.2637	0.4692	0.6821	1.0000	
More than WTP-60	0.0089	0.2171	0.3863	0.5616	0.8233	1.0000

N=200

The Table 9 shows that household monthly income is highly correlated with willingness to pay. Visitors with higher household monthly income there is a probability to pay higher than those household with lower income.

Figure 1 Inverse Demand Curve for Dhaka Zoo respondent visitors through Willingness to Pay Bidding

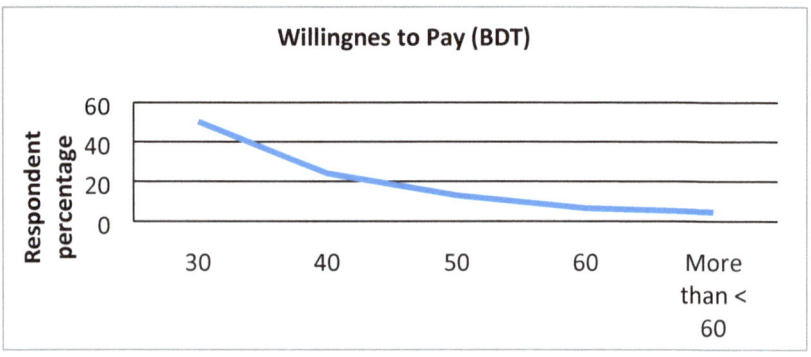

The *Figure 1* above shows an inverse demand curve for visits to Dhaka Zoo. Around 50 per cent respondents mentioned that they were willing to pay BDT 30 as entry fee, while this reduces to only 4.5 per cent respondents who were willing to pay more than BDT 60 as entry fee.

Table 10 Suggestions for Improvements of Current Situation

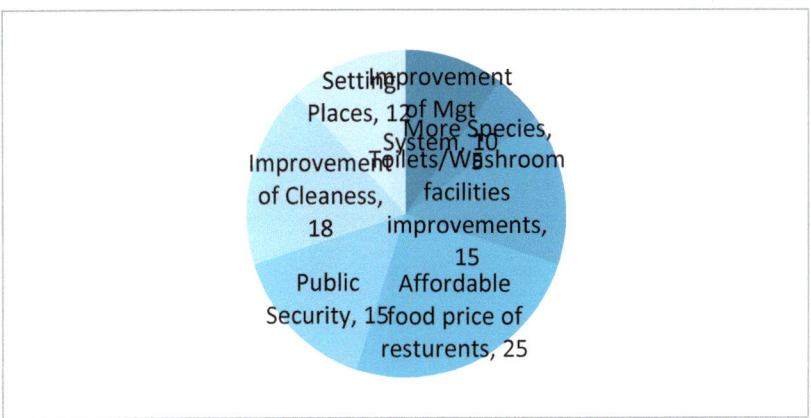

The *Table 10* above shows the result that *sample respondents identified major problems and lackings they have faced during Dhaka Zoo visit. Which sectors should government give more emphasis for improvement of current situation of Dhaka Zoo.High price of fast food and snacks items under the resturents of Dhaka Zoo should bring under restriction suggested by 25 per cent respondents,Improve cleaness of Zoo suggested by 18 per cent respondents,More washroom facilities demanded by 15 per cent respondents, Increase public security by 15 per cent respondents,Improvement of*

tatal management service of Dhaka Zoo by 10 per cent respondents, More setting places and more species demanded by 12 per cent and 5 per cent respondents respectively.

Table 11 Ways of Financing Dhaka Zoo for Improvements from Current Situation

Proposed Ways of Financing	Per cent
	Single opinion for financing
Raise the entry fees	6
Raise govrnment budget	15
Corporate Social responsibility (CSR)/Donation	15
	Combined openion for financing
Raise the entry fees and raise govt. budget	6
Raise the entry fees and Corporate Social responsibility (CSR)/Donation	11
Raise govrnment budget and Corporate Social responsibility (CSR)/Donation	47
Total	100

The above *Table 11* exhibits that, In our survey we asked repodent visitors to give their openion for financing Dhaka Zoo to improve current situation to overcome those problems they have faced during zoo visit.Where 36 per cent have proposed single opinion for way of financing.Where 64 per cent proposed combined way of financing.

8. Policy Recommendations and Implications

The Dhaka Zoo has great potential and huge economic values for whole country. Such as these suggestions below for future development plans will require for long term commitment by the government.

- Current entry fee is 20 Taka.The entry fee to the zoo may be adjusted gradually matching with inflation. This would generate additional revenue to cover the operating and maintenance expenses of the zoo. This study suggests that people would be willing to pay a higher entry fee for the zoo. Yet, an increase in entry fee will reduce the consumer surplus for the visitors.

- Since visitors to the zoo come from a variety of income groups, the zoo may consider developing several levels of service with gradually higher fees. A self guided tour could be introduced with briefing at the information center that will help the visitors make a better plan. The idea is to cater to the needs of the visitors of differing socioeconomic and cultural backgrounds.

- Two restaurants (mainly first food) and two souvenir shops were found closed. Authority said that price of all food items are fixed and price list are displayed in front of restaurant but actually visitors were alleged to having to pay higher prices. This is an example of slack of supervision on behalf of the administration.

- The surrounding environment of the zoo was found to be unclean. With small improvements in administrative control, things could improve.

- There are few poorly maintained rest rooms for women and children. More washroom facilities are needed.

- Public security is not sufficient enough within the zoo, visitors face harassments due to limited security guard for their protection.

- Absence of animal waste management facility is a cause of concern since this causes harm both for visitors and animals as well.

- Government can introduce luxury bus service within Dhaka City to get to the zoo. The buses currently in operation are less likely to attract people of middle and higher income groups. In different occasions Dhaka Zoo can offer package tours in collaboration with travel agencies for large groups and distant visitors cause the study findings indicate that people are willing to pay a high enough price to render these feasible.

In conclusion, the information in this study on willingness to pay, composition of visitors by income, mode of transportation used, and features of attraction should be used in the national budget, in preparing development plans for the zoo, in identifying areas of weaknesses, and assessing the benefits derived from the Dhaka Zoological Garden.

References

(1) Brander, L. M., J. G. Raymond, M. Florax and J. E. Vermaat (2006), The empirics of wetland valuation: a comprehensive summary and a meta–analysis of the literature, *Environmental and Resource Economics* 33: 223-250

(2) B,Malakar, M,Khan and L,Chakraborty (2010) The Zoo As Ecotourism Attraction- Visitor Reactions And Perceptions: The Case Of Dhaka Zoo, Bangladesh

(3) Bowker, J. M. and V. R. Leeworthy (1998), 'Accounting for ethnicity in recreation demand: a cost demand studies', *American Journal of Agricultural Economics* 68(3) : 660-667 flexible count data approach', *Journal of Leisure Resea*rch 30

(4) F.A. Ward, D.J .Beal – (2000), Valuing nature with travel cost models: A manual.

(5) Freeman, A. Myrick III (1993), *The Measurement of Environmental and Resource Values: Theory and Methods,* Washington, D.C: Resources for the Future

(6) Garrod, Guy and K.G. Willis (1999), *Economic Valuation of the Environment: Methods and Case Studies,* Cheltenham, UK and Northampton, MA, USA: Edward Elgar.

(7) Gunatilake, H. M. (2003), *Environmental Valuation: Theory and Applications*, Peradeniya: Post Graduate Institute of Agriculture, University of Peradeniya, Sri Lanka.

(8) Gunatilake, H. M. and G. R. Vieth (1998), An assessment of scenic value of Sri Lankan elephants in case of Pinnawela orphanage, *Sri Lankan Journal of Social Sciences* 21(182): 37-57.

(9) Grigalunas, T., J. Opaluch and S. Trandafir (2004), *Non-Market Benefits and Cost of Preserving Estuarine Watershed Open Space: A Case Study of Riverhead,* Long Island, NY: Economic Analysis Inc.

(10) Hanker, N., et al., (1997), Willingness to Pay for Borivli National Park: Evidence from a Contingent Valuation, Ecological Economics, 105-122. Isangkura, A. (1998), Environmental Valuation: An Entrance Fee System for National Parks in Thailand.

(11) Hanley, N and Spash, C. L., 1993. Cost-Benefit Analysis and the Environment. (London: Edward Elgar Publishing, Ltd.

(12) Hotelling, H. (1947), The Economics of Public Recreation: The Prewitt Report, Washington, D.C: National Park Services.

(13) Kaosa-ard, M., D. Patmasiriwat, T. Panayotou, and J.R. Deshazo (1995), Green Financing: Valuation and Financing of Khao Yai National Park in Thailand, Thailand Development Research Institute, Bangkok.

(14) Kealy, M. J. and R. C. Bishop (1986), Theoretical and empirical specifications issues in travel.

(15) Khan.H, April 2004. Demand for Eco-tourism: Estimating Recreational Benefits from the Margalla Hills National Park in Northern Pakistan, (SANDEE).

(16) Lindberg, K. and R.L. Johnson (1994), Estimating Demand for Ecotourism Sites in Developing Nations Trends, 31: 10-15.

(17) Loomis, J.B. and R.G. Walsh (1997), Recreation Economic Decisions: Comparing Benefits and Costs, Venture Publishing, State College, PA.

(18) McKean, J.R., D.M. Johnson and R.G. Walsh (1995), 'Valuing Time in Travel Cost Demand Analysis: An Empirical Investigation' Land Economics, 71 (1): 96 105.

(19) Ministry of Fisheries and Livestock, Government of the People's Republic of Bangladesh. (www.mofl.gov.bd) and Dhaka Zoo curator office.

(20) Munganata, E.D. and S. Navrud (1994), Environmental Valuation in Developing Countries: The Recreational Value of Wildlife Viewing', *Ecological Economics,* 11: 135-51. Nillesen, E. (2002).

(21) Nam, P. K., T. V. H. Son and H. Cesar (2005), '=Economic valuation of the Hon Mun marine protected area, Working Paper

05/13, Poverty Reduction and Environmental Management (PREM).

(22) Parsons, G. R. (2003), The travel cost model, in P. A. Champ, K. J. Boyle, and T. C. Brown (eds.), *A Primer on Nonmarket Valuation,* London: Kluwer Academic Publishing.

(23) Poor, P. J. and J. M. Smith (2004), Travel cost analysis of a cultural heritage site: the case of historic St. Mary's City of Maryland, *Journal of Cultural Economics. Page 28(3)*

(24) Rolfe, J. and P. Prabha (2007), Estimating values for recreational fishing at freshwater dams in Queensland, *The Australian Journal of Agricultural and Resource Economics* 51(2).

(25) Shammin, Md. Rumi (1999), Application of the travel cost method (TCM): A case study of environmental valuation of Dhaka zoological garden . *IUCN*

(26) S.S Shinwary, M.J .Rahman and M,Uddin (2009), Zoo as Ecotourism Attraction–Case of Dhaka Zoo.

(27) T,Monoj and M ,Thusitha (2010), To Develop Or to Conserve ? The Case of the Diyawanna Oya Wetlands in Sri Lanka.

Abbreviations and acronym

ITCM=Individuals Travel Cost Method

ZTCM = Zonal Travel Cost Method

CE = Choice Experiments

CEF = Conditional Expenditure Function

CS =Consumer Surplus

CV = Contingent Valuation

CVM = Contingent Valuation Method

WTA/ WTAC = Willingness to Accept /Compensation

WTP = Willingness to Pay

SB=Social Benefit

SC=Social Cost

$ = US Dollar

BDT=Bangladesh Taka

TCM= Travel Cost Method

HPF=Household production function

TGF=Trip Generating Function

Envq= Environmental quality

WAZA=World Association of Zoos and Aquariums

LoYV =Last one year visitation

ANNEX

Dhaka Zoo in the Region

www.ingramcontent.com/pod-product-compliance
Lightning Source LLC
Chambersburg PA
CBHW050851290526
45792CB00002B/606